BOOKS & PAMPHLETS BY DAVID BROMIGE:

1965 *The Gathering* (Poems & prose, 1962-65)
    Sumbooks Press, Buffalo

1968 *Please, Like Me* (Poetry)
    Black Sparrow Press, LA

1968 *The Ends of the Earth* (Poems, 1965-68)
    Black Sparrow Press, LA

1969 *The Quivering Roadway* (Poetry)
    Archangel Press, Berkeley

1971 *Threads* (Poems, 1968-70)
    Black Sparrow Press, LA

1971 *The Fact So Of Itself* (with Robert Kelly & Diane
    Wakoski) (Poetry)
    Black Sparrow Press, LA

1973 *Three Stories*
    Black Sparrow Press, LA

1973 *Ten Years in the Making* (Selected poems, songs
    & stories, 1961-70)
    New Star Press, Vancouver

1974 *Birds of the West* (Poems, 1970-72)
    Coachhouse Press, Toronto

1974 *Tight Corners & What's Around Them*
    (Poems & prose, 1972-73)
    Black Sparrow Press, LA

1974 *Spells & Blessings* (Poetry)
    Talonbooks, Vancouver

1974 *Out of My Hands* (Prose)
    Black Sparrow Press, LA

TIGHT CORNERS & WHAT'S AROUND THEM *(being the brief & endless adventures of some pronouns in the sentences of 1972-1973)* Prose and Poems by DAVID BROMIGE

Black Sparrow Press • *Los Angeles* • *1974*

Some of this writing first appeared in these magazines: *Buttons,
Ear In The Wheatfield, Earthship, The End In Itself, The Falcon,
Occident, Open Hand, Open Reading, Paper Pudding, Poetry Re-
view, The Sonoma Review, Sparrow, Spectrum, This,* and *Vort.*

LIBRARY OF CONGRESS CATALOGING IN PUBLICATION DATA

Bromige, David
    Tight corners & what's around them.

    I. Title.
PS3552.R635T53   811'.5'4   74-8470
ISBN 0-87685-194-4
ISBN 0-87685-193-6 (pbk.)

to Tom Sharp
for his carpentry

to several more
for their intensities

who'll identify themselves
for sure

to Sherril Jaffe
that's for sure

CONTENT.

ANGLING

O such themes—equalities! O divine average!
Walt Whitman, "Starting from Paumanok"

Circular motion symbolizes faultless activity.
Laurence Binyon, his final footnote to
his translation of *The Divine Comedy*

Around an appearance, one common model, we grow up many.
Charles Olson, "The Kingfishers"

No man shall be an idiot for purely exterior reasons.
Robert Creeley, "The Rites"

To know the future would be the death of our souls.
Karl Jaspers, *Origin & Goal of History*

It's becoming plainer every day that Breton's "future resolution of the states of dream and reality" is no longer just around the corner.
John Ashbery

Came, came.
Came a word, came,
came through the night,
wanted to glow, wanted to glow.
Paul Celan, "Engführung"

TIGHT CORNERS

&

WHAT'S AROUND THEM

THEY ARE EYES

They arise
intent on us
& their intent's
that we do good,

thus, to this end,
by being small,
they make us spacious
so that we know scope,

& are circular & flat
to make us know
how round & tall we are,
like wells, we are to lean into

to drink, & dip up
water for our brothers
& our sisters too—
they shine

not alone to say
Let your gleam be revealed
but to remind us of the darkness
each encloses—

aren't they enormous also
to help us in our knowing
of ant or bee or
cell of our own body,

& to warn us
we can be mistaken,
& more than one can count
or even see, because

if a body lose
awareness of its weight
among the billions of its kind
its life will waste—

& they are blind
to remind us
each is
singular,

& to insist, You must
use your mind to make believe
the stories of the real you tell
are true, & to that end

they constellate.

FOR SAN ANTONIO ESTERO

Such scenery wasn't always thought appealing. They found it lovely because it looked like pictures they had been told were so? As for the exercise, that could be had on any city block. The developers had already blazed a road over the hills to this valley. How lone it was, the estuary birds & a few sheep the only moving things beside themselves. It spoke to his soul. When would his soul fill up with houses, & catch up with the world he was born into. He watched the contractor's truck moving down the dirt road across the river. He hated whatever was driving it. He wanted the whole earth to return to the condition of this valley. His soul *was* filled with vast tracts of houses & demanded purgation. He thought how, as a boy, only a few kids in any place had come in close, the rest a background music, unavoidable nuisances, or threats. He too was a nuisance, for he lived in a house, a hateful thing upon the grandeur of the earth's aloneness—a lonesome creature grand in its self-loathing, craving release to some simpler time, when emptiness was to be filled, not treasured as a no-man's-land to keep anguish homeless. Perhaps only the vastness of the prospect encouraged such abstraction. If he looked in front of him, climbing, he saw only innumerable blades of grass & a lot of grasshoppers.

UNDER FLUORESCENT LIGHTS
(after *Fantasia of the Unconscious*)

Under fluorescent lights the voice is pitched high, starting from
the larynx & resonating thinly in the maxillary sinoid cavities.
By candlelight, the conditions otherwise unaltered, the voice is
pitched considerably lower, rising from the diaphragm & resonat-
ing in the upper chest, the region of the great plexus of symp-
athetic feeling. The content of what's said is more kindly, painful
to hear perhaps but spoken from the heart, sans the insincerities
that so often shrill out of the cheeks & nose.

Sunlight, where the body of the speaker's exposed to its warmth
also, will locate the voice deep in the diaphragm, lulling the
thoracic ganglion, foscussing sensation in the, solar, plexus. An
animal sureness of relaxation informs our speech.

But today clouds beyond our volition make that impossible. How-
ever, anyone can light a candle or flick a switch, giving the other
great truths their location.

Sir Bernard said
We are happy to join in
In this new era

Initiating observations
That would not be possible
But for political   & milit'ry   divisions

Forcing governments to an expenditure
That never would be borne
As a budget for fundamental scientific work alone

The successes of the USSR in this work
The single-minded purpose
Carried through with human welfare taking second place

The direct continuous communication
Between the Council of Ministers & the senior Academicians
Determines that no human frailities or vacillations

Shall interfere with   this unity of purpose
Unparalleled in Western life
He said   Oort & his staff   This in the Low Countries

Produced results of almost unbelievable
Detail & elegance describing parts
Parts of the Milky Way which man will never see

Clouds of interstellar dust obscure the view from telescopes
It is charact'ristic of man's skill
That today we have partially restored our ego

Devising means to penetrate this dust
The light & radio waves by which we make our study
Set out many million years ago   At present

The limit of our observations
Is our information
Several thousand million years behind

The conditions which existed then
Are crucially important to the question
What is our universe's origin

What shall it become   You'll understand
That those who seek this knowledge
Seize any prospects of surmounting

The hindrances of our environment
With a particular passion   Today
The radio went on   The air's alive

With a new expectancy & hope
Because our instruments may be   Reaching so far out
In space that soon we may

Be able to speak with greater confidence
He said   In a billion years the universe
Will look to us

To us   Much as it does now
You will appreciate that my own life
Determines a particular outlook

TWICE I HAD BEEN SURE

Twice I had been sure—
was every day to be a torment
spent negotiating with the prey
these smokes of chance would drive my way—
these people, entities
that is, opaque with motive
as they are impure?
Daylight is pale beside my mind, I fought
to find the fire behind its pall,
locating it where centuries before
saints, heretics & witches blazed with it,
before the sickly illumination broke
that spoke of certainty
as merely probable,
save in the womb or thrusting forth from it—

& hadn't they pointed out the way I was
to save them by, worshipers of sureness
as each one was, though now they called it
energy, & waited on a judge—
so I saw God in them, or saw the Devil,
& all each person thought to say
to temper good or evil
like fat or muscle fell away
in sizzling sentences to feed the flames
whose glare reveals the soul—

the trust I offered them they offered me
hesitancy in return for, my stare
met only faltering glances as my nostrils flared
to breathe that stink of fear—
if a woman let me in
acknowledging my right
still her tissue must betray us both
since other cocks could cause delight's
illusions to suffuse it, mocking mine
unless her mortal part fused at the martyr's stake—
if she refused me,
deluded in her notion of the good,
so that I fell throughout the night alone,

once she had seen in me her guilt & doubt,
my star became an ember in the hell she made
until those tears of penitence
burst from her veins, but my just vengeance
I exacted in fantasy alone, this was the only evil—

this, & all my life between
corrupted with perspectives
they'd invented, this *they* whose particles of fear
disguise & violate what holds them here, the sphere,
as though the source of life
depended on an Earth for sustenance—!

They had invented too
what they then treated with as *me,*
& my terror as I saw this falseness fall away
from what in truth I was
was all the force
I conjured with to penetrate the flesh
& cause the blood to flow
as the human body parted to admit me
& I was free to go.

THE PROTESTANT POEM

The lifemaster's an ideal human being
He reveals the path one has to follow
He takes one's life into his keeping

A sentence shows the words the way to go
Although a sentence needs the help of words
It holds their sense within its keeping

The first sentences we learn we learn as wholes
Most likely when we're in our parents' keeping
Then as we grow they're built up out of parts

But a sentence is imperfect
In what sense is a sentence so
In the sense that language is

Doubly indeterminate   We must rely both on
Its formalism   Parenthesis
For words are shorthand   Words make a kind of code

Words are akin to LCDs
We must rely on them to speak   Thus
Close the parenthesis two lines above

We must rely as well upon our own
Continued reconsideration
Of how this formalism has a bearing on our own

Experience   Just as   since our knowledge
Is ultimately tacit   we can never say
All that we know   just so

Since the character of meaning's also tacit
Ultimately   we can never know all we imply
In what we say   But this ideal

Human   This lifemaster
Instructs   by acts of a nonverbal character also
Actions speak as loud as words   or louder

This might mean they shout
As if in triumph at one's recognition
That the path one has to follow

Through this kaleidoscopic world
Was revealed to one by them
The subject of that sentence

That opens with a shout
Is difficult to find   but anyone
Might find   oneself   the object

This is a peril of the language
He must use to tell me of his lifemaster
This ideal human being

Who must use language too
Though not without corroboration
A way of life acts as a demonstration

Actions constitute a language of their own
We can read meaning in a person's every deed
Each silence   immobile if he be   amid our flux

And since the world like a kaleidoscope
A huge kaleidoscope
And one one cannot step out of to shake

So much for simile   never
Can repeat a previous pattern absolutely
We can achieve consistency

Only by identifying manifestly different situations
In respect of some particular   and this
Requires our judgment

Our personal decision
We are persons   This necessitates a series
Never-ending   of each person's judgments

To judge implies that one can be mistaken
You could be wrong   I might   Or he or she
That possibility is always present

Unless one is an ideal human being
A lifemaster who'll reveal to his disciple
That the disciple's judged correctly

The disciple who must judge he's found the one
Who will reveal to him
That he has judged correctly

(some of this language comes from Michael
Polanyi's *Personal Knowledge*)

He was to go into his feelings that he avoided so adroitly with thought. When he asked his thought for a picture he was shown the crawl-space underneath the house, where he had never been & where he had no intention of going if he could possibly help it. Going into it a little further he found there were cobwebs against his face, spiders he couldn't quite see, & knew these were only tokens of what wouldn't present itself in the picture. He sat in the living room, lit by four standing lamps of considerable elegance, astutely placed, both for use & for effect; the hardwood floor shone, the furniture made all kinds of sense. Leave this for the darkness & confusion that, by being underneath, in a sense made *this* room possible?

Now he was arguing towards a glimpsed conclusion, moving a lamp a little nearer to his questioner's person, wanting, he remarked, to see her better, & coincidentally dazzling her. If that place made this one possible, then hadn't he made the right decision, to experience *it here*, to stay where he was, leaving the other area to be the living room of what more properly dwelt there—black imaginary widows &, in short, the unthinkable?

Yet he was intrigued with what she had to present, & this argued a certain pain, for if utter satisfaction were his, wouldn't he fall asleep—wouldn't he be, already, asleep? Still, if this was a dream, it was one that pressed toward its end. If you hurt bad enough, a memory of a friend who had started to be shrunk told him, You go. But it was *his* notion that madness inhered in deliberately going out, into the night, then down the steps & on his hands & knees to crawl through the darker veil that was the entrance, down there. Sooner or later, he knew, he would get up to cross this floor & it would simply give way beneath him, not because it was rotten but because it was a picture, & you can't walk about in a picture. He would be plunged into the underneath before he had to think about it & that would be that. Nothing left to do at that point but scream.

But this would probably not happen today, or even this week. He would suffuse himself with terror, screaming for help & screaming at anyone crazy enough to pull him out. So in this way too he would not have to look at the crawl-space.

He now thought this was not only beneath him in space but be-
hind him in time, & so far back that his success at survival
throughout the years argued against the necessity of exploration.
But she now drew to his attention the fact that, upstairs, there
was another crawl-space. So the house, which looks so spacious
from outside, is, as far as its liveable portions go, almost
cramped.

Was it love, he wondered, made him listen to this uncomfortable
guest—if, first & last, love for himself? But love is blind so why
not stay put or, say, move the whole show into the next room,
where the bed was. The sexual charge was a welling up of the
otherwise inadmissable—so he had conceived. What if he were to
enter her own crawl-space with a cool expectation of suffering—
suffering all corners & each fold with a deliberation possibly pas-
sionate but divorced from the enchantment he desired to feel
but that was, after all, only a web of thought—for such, he fig-
ured, was fantasy. In fantasy also he saw what memory called
Th'expense of spirit in a waste of shame. But love! he balked,
closing his eyes. These were his own lids naturally, over his own
eyeballs.

One must love from strength not weakness. He opened them up
& looked into hers, green where there is color to be refused but,
as everywhere, darkly open at center. The hero has a thousand
faces but he would be all alone in the basement. Is it weak to
want to fuse one's being with another's. Were the pictures on
these walls to relieve the monotony or was analogy one more
evasion.

The fact of it is, there is two thousand dollars' worth of dryrot
under this house, & somebody is going to have to do something
about it. But it's all a fiction since I sit here writing of it, & facts
do not enter such writing without undergoing transformation.
There is the time of writing having energies specific to itself that
preoccupation by what earlier occurred transgresses. Thinking
this made him uneasy. Calling himself *him* helped, if only from a
distance. She sat, after all, some little distance from him. And
upstairs, when one came to read this, it would be the same.

If he sat in the room, wasn't that what he had to confront—sitting there trying not to be filled with the other place. There, he would not be able to look at her, & her visible presence was part of her persuasiveness. She had persuaded him to recognize the act that charged his feelings so—it was something done to him so terrible, so heartrending, that it was unavengeable. He would do anything to revenge himself, he thought, & thought—thinking, that the child was someone he no longer was, it had been done to another person altogether. He was crying, suddenly, grief forcing itself up from the darkness in his chest, blurring his eyes. But you are crying for yourself, he imagined she had said. And the light was back.

Concepts protect us from experience. So she had conceived.

She was urging him to seize the day, to see his hour had come, there would be no second chance, he would forever be a weak creature if he didn't stand on his own two feet. She leaned on him as she spoke, but then too he was half-supported by her. Now her husband was tugging at her sleeve, saying just a minute. The man, startled, said Whose minute.

Faceless Fussduck put away his dry revolver. The closet was wet.

27

What worried him was, that he would not for long be able to put up with the ways life would be. Appealing as he found a number of people, not one but turned out discomfortingly weird in one way or another—what was it, as though some vast chord of madness had been struck on some unimaginable piano, & each were a wire, reverberating. Not that he couldn't see it with some clarity—a darkwood upright floating somewhere between Mars & Venus, a man in tails playing it, his patent-leather pumps at its pedals. But enough of facts. Why give so much of our belief to that which can be proven to be true. It was not *his* faith that was in question. He addressed himself once more to the visitor, & agreed that there seemed little likelihood of physical death destroying the essential character of the deceased. Then he asked him, if he liked piano music.

She asked him how he felt about their relationship. When the light's out in your fridge, how do you know if the door's open. Speech is a relief at such times. He said the first thing that came into his head. Then he tried to follow where it led. That was how they'd met. Apparently it led to the refrigerator. Apparently there was nothing she wanted to eat right then.

She had fucked him over he said. Faceless Fussduck slapped
him on the back for the second time. He had begun to duck &
the blow caught him behind the ear, clouding his thought.
Hold still, he was ordered, I can explain it all, his advisor
added. The dishes, furniture & books had been divided up
before he got home. He had fallen into the hands of a Terrible
mother.

She gave him sound advice—now he knew, when he wanted to
be himself, who to stay away from.

But what is to stop them, it might be asked, from spending
their whole lives lying about like the beasts in the field or the
ladies in the pornographic stories, perpetually ready to receive
the advances made upon them. The answer is—nothing.

The scenario was rehearsed for a month in a stage-set replica of the objective on the Florida Gulf Coast. When we realized there was no-one in the compound, it was like hollering in an empty room, I had the most horrible feeling of my life. All the courage, the long training, the perfectly executed mission, had come to naught. The Secretary of Defense was moved to declare the Son Tay affair a successfully completed operation.

4 FOR THE BATTLE OF BRITAIN

Lord Astor had said that London could take it.

In about 6 hours I'm going to drop these, Kenney said. Do you want to send a message to anyone in Germany. Sure, I told him, & I took out a pencil & wrote on the bright yellow side of one, Love & kisses. Under that I signed my name.

It had been a wonderful zoo, but those in charge were afraid that the repercussion from the bombs might blast open the cages, resulting in the animals' finding themselves loose.

In the square facing the House & Westminster Abbey there was a huge statue of Abraham Lincoln. It was comforting to see the strong face of Lincoln there that morning. Probably he understood why the Germans had bombed the House of Commons & Westminster Abbey.

Contemplating what had to be taken apart & erected, he sensed the nearness to despair. If only he were to make the materials somehow bigger,—stretched so that fewer of them would suffice. But on that rack would their information lose integrity. On that rack he himself would confess to anything, just to be done with it. What was needed was to keep the materials intact, stretching, instead, the edifice, so that it would have to contain more space than he'd supposed. Again, though, time itself could be stretched, that is, its integrity could be preserved, for in stretching it he meant only that the project should be longer. It could not be cut off by death because with each act of dismantling & reconstruction the whole assumed, again, a final shape. So, then—it looked like everything was fine after all which was a relief because it was getting very late & he was mainly concerned with the evasion of despair.

When irritated, he may form an hypothesis. He scratches energetically, but it takes time & requires a surface. On this the blister is raised. Luckily, when it breaks scar tissue forms, as if in answer to the real possibility of infection from without. When the scab drops off, the bacteria are still present, but the mosquitoes come & go, consuming & producing, laid & hatched in the swamp of the soul. He was of an irritable nature before he'd encountered their similes.

31

Their necks had not been gradually elongating; their lips had not grown harder, nor more prominent; their legs & feet were not daily altering their shape; their hair was not beginning to resemble feathery stubs; thus you would think it obvious that these were not ostriches but people.

Because it's small, relatively inexpensive & easily introduced into a room, it may serve as a model to demonstrate the universe. If a pin is inserted into this integument, a sudden deflation will occur.

As he walked by, for the umpteenth time, the dogs started their barking. It would take a Pavlov to teach them any different. Their heads could be removed from their bodies & someone else could do the barking.

I wanted to worship you. I wanted to send you on ahead. I wanted to send you on a head on a platter.

Having thinking as my inferior function, I fell under the sway of Jung's "Psychological Types."

We can send someone in your place, they assured him. Great, & who was it. You, they replied.

I had to fill out the form in duplicate. I didn't. I didn't.

The 4 young rock musicians, hoping to scale the Beetling cliffs, so to speak, contrive to be filmed chasing birds through swinging London. The movie idles with the Id, ergo the Egoism is exaggerated, while the conception is Super. Now the girls have hopped on a bus, then steal a car you idiots. Take advantage of them. It's only a fuckin flick.

Think of the truth. Think about poetry. Imagine a number. Double it. Add too. Halve what now you have. Surrender the figure you first thought of & your answer's won.

Now it had been done crooked & would have to be done all over again. Now it had been done crooked & would have to be done all over again. Now it had been done crooked & would have to be done all over again.

Plus ce change, plus le meme chose, & he's sure nothing has changed here.

Along with the phone they had installed a device to allow them to turn down the bell. Should it be used, no matter how urgent or trivial the message, it would not get through, because they wouldn't hear the signal that preceded it. It would only be as though they were out of the house, or in a coma, or dead. When they were dead news, no matter how alarming, would no longer concern them. But they were not yet dead, & so could move from place to place, raise their arms, bend the fingers, appose the thumbs, & switch it off or on.

He had gotten ahold of one of the oldest of philosophical con-
troversies. Or had it gotten ahold of him. Without further ado
he started in to write. Which was the primary impulse.

Her misery was real & to do with the fear that others would
manipulate her. When she first came to Free House, she wasn't
at all sure she trusted the inmates. But shortly she found they
would give her what she wanted, & she waited on those above
her without fear or favor.

I'm half-woman myself. My mother was one. My father also had a mother. But was she any more to be trusted than my own? Both were of mixed blood. Men & women will try by all means possible to cope with its insistence that its mixing continue, even to the betrayal of their sexuality.

Were these people really all walking around with bags over their heads? When you start to doubt your own skepticism, look out!

So you think there may be something to astrology
That human life to some degree or other
Must be influenced by planets & by stars

Though not completely
A range remains
A range for human action originating in oneself

Inspired by others probably
In response to other humans I expect
One way or another

You think that force from outer space
To some extent determines human fate
And by studying the lore

By applying one's mind to the records
Human beings have been keeping down the years
Each in his own time & place   Own language

Each in the year that that recorder was alive
Moving among his or her own kind
One can read how forces such as these

Influence behavior
So that a system one believes in operates
Assuring us both by   & of   its constancy

It's an attractive proposition
Not easy to discount
One can laugh at it but will it go away

A system of belief that has persisted as it has
Why shouldn't there be something to it
The moon pulls at the oceans & the land

We know the sun is source of all
Our all   How like these are to a planet & a star
How small they are compared to most

Of course they're relatively close
Humans have imagined them as wife & husband
Sun & daughter   Relatively

Each is close to us as a husband or a wife
Relative to men & women who aren't cohabiting with one
Or won't   Or can't   Or haven't for a while

Desire can see the outlines of the furthest mountain
But love is blind
One sees the Earth with fresh eyes from the moon

But few can have that chance
But from the furthest mountain roundabout
Our valley is disclosed anew

Why couldn't there be something to it
Perhaps it isn't true   It's valid though
Given the initial premise

Given that some heavenly body
Apparently remote
Could in a sense be thought to show an interest

Who wouldn't fall to plotting
Become familiar with its course
Its customary haunts   Already in its power

Though we don't have all the facts in yet
Not all the counters have revealed themselves
We must make do with what we've got   Thus far

Once upon a time   In fact
Once upon a New Years Eve   The eve of 1800
Piazzi saw a star   It was quite small

Not catalogued   His heart leapt up
In the constellation Taurus
He called it Ceres

Though it was the first
Olbers took the next step
Using the ephemeris of Gauss

On March 28   1802   Not too far from Ceres
In his line of sight
A second planet in the gap

The so-called gap
Between Jupiter & Mars
Olbers wrote to Bode

Did Pallas & Ceres always travel in their current orbits
In peaceful proximation
Or are both debris of a former & a larger planet

Which exploded   Huth
Thought not   His mind was quite made up
Maybe he was right   I can't decide

These tiny planets are as old as all the others
The matter they are formed of
Coagulated   Forming many such small spheres

Not much time passed   Relatively speaking
Before astronomers began to tire of their profusion
Said one who has remained anonymous

Nonetheless we know his thoughts on this
One planetoid was a sensation
A dozen fine

Fifty were still interesting
Today I call them Vermin of the skies
Their number now is estimated to be 30,000

Or more than 30,000
We do not find them mentioned
In the ancients   Their lore doesn't exist

Except in recent books
Take Hermes for example
Astronomers could not give absolute assurance

That a body such as Hermes might not run into the Earth
In December 1937 Hermes passed the Earth
At a distance somewhat under 500,000 miles

This was not the closest that it could have come
It could have come as close as 220,000
Closer than the moon

Was it trying to tell us something   Huh
That's up to us   Right now I notice how it didn't
Violate our boundaries   In a sense it did

With what anguish many must have waited
In Hell nor were they out of it
Until the future came to pass   And Hermes guided them

Are they to blame   It weighs 3000 million tons
Tiny for a planetoid   But many times the mass
Of the object which caused the mile-wide impact crater

Out in Arizona
What object   That object whose impact on what's known
        as Arizona
That crater tells us of

41

How to re-write the lore of planetary influence
Now that the planetoids are here to stay
And always were

Since at least 100 million years ago
About the time that flowers appeared on Earth
Flowers   Which Darwin called an abominable mystery

They spread so fast
Appeared so suddenly
Like the human beings their appearance is associated with

No doubt these asteroids or planetoids
Shed their rays upon our Earth
Exerted & exert their subtle influences

Hundreds of astronomers will testify to this
Since 1800
To their influence on human actions

Thought is action of a sort
And speech   Sad not to have a tape
An interview with Shakespeare   Dante

Reading in Italian
Thought that doesn't come to action though   Beyond its brain
Does it leave a trace

Fine indentations on the brainpan possibly
On cerebella long returned to earth
Such is our lot   We come back to earth

Writing is an act
Writing makes a kind of record
The records our astrology is founded on

These are written records in the main
Imperfect though
They leave a gap unfilled

The story of the planetoids
Of their effect on our behavior
This gap makes a kind of crater

What thoughts belong to them
Perhaps a pattern will appear
This present writing springs from them

But can influence be willed
It's more a matter of what dreams have they inspired
Since the explosion

The explosions   Hirayama
Thought there'd been not one but five
Each causing what already had been called a family

Because its members moved in similar orbits
Perhaps a complex of such patterns might be traced
Maybe direct examination of a planetoid

Will provide a clue   Eros
Is most likely Willy Ley believes
His book   Watchers of the Skies

Is cited here   He means astronomers
But each of us looks up from time to time
Struck with the beauty   Our souls are amplified

It's hard to stop
Harder to bear sometimes
And then this faculty can rescue us

And take us to its heavens
At times the stars   Venus   Mars   gleam through
At times shine on a pattern

Perhaps the truth that they appear to point to
Is recorded by the watchers
Of the postures of the watchers of the skies

THE FUTURE IS OUR MOTHER

Constantly she gives us birth.
We read in where we've been
what we are constantly
about to be.   Flesh
as she is.   In action
each is born anew
when the future is behind us.
And if it's all too much for one
then back into the womb one tries to go.

ON A PHOTOGRAPH FROM CHILDHOOD:
OF MY MOTHER, MY SISTER, & ME

Everything happens for the first time ever.
That's how we recognize it.   When we do
that's how come we smile like that
& how come I can say
that's what this picture's saying:
the Lord, they say, will know his own.

These dispositions of the dark & light
in print
keep faith
the mind needs for its ease
& what we saw then
we see now
except for her who held us
who has met it
yet dreams on with her arms around us
assured we'll be together
once again.

I KNOW

I know we'll make love this Wednesday.
I know I've often been mistaken.
I know hope springs eternal but
forget how it goes on.

I know disappointment makes me bitter.
I know why love is said
to make the world go round.
I know other ways to say this.

I know there's no going back,
no other way to say this.
I know how we'll caress & this
is how I know.

WISDOM KNOWS
(for David Weiner)

Wisdom knows
its moon shines on
the topside of these clouds

Its light reveals apparent error,
telling us that, No, it's so,
on any night, someplace wisdom knows.

SOUL MATES

The plague had been upon the land before he arrived but he had to be responsible for it. He plucked out both his eyes. Four more grew in his head & his responsibility doubled. He grew twice as lonely & his despair led him to tear off both ears. Now he would not have to attend to their accusations. But the expected happened & rather than speak of that he tore out his tongue. But there were already more than enough mouths to be fed. He became a member of a group dedicated to feeding them & immediately the number of groups dedicated to starving them doubled. He dug a hole thinking to pull it in after him but someone up & died in the one next to it & he lost his grip. He might as well wish upon a star at this point to get him out, but which one? In the morning his arms were discovered frozen in the attitudes of prayers. The suns rose, the arms thawed & fell off. Now he had four & using two to hold his head, he cut it off with the other two. He would never be alone again. He was terrified the other head already had the plague, & that was how this thought got into whichever was his. Whichever was his. He had to be responsible for it. The plague had been upon the land before he arrived.

LET THEM

Let her let him kiss her
though she considers him repulsive
so she worries what to do next time she meets him,
let her cure herself of her habits of submission.
Even though I am her husband
desire recognizes many women
my fantasies press up against me
every bit as willing as I make them
I push them away with constancy
that's what they pull me with—
I want to say I understand that man.
What's more seductive than integrity.

"THAT RUSH, THAT ALWAYS"

That rush, that always
precedes the wave or wall of fog,
drives air too fast into our lungs—

You wanted breath,
you got it—how
should the wind

measure what it is in discrete sounds,
the words are mine,
are ours.   They'll tell

how the landscape vanishes
except a kind of moving circle
we follow to get home.   The wind

will drop, predictably.
These elemental forces
stir us in themselves,

how should they mean more than they are,
we say, natural phenomena—
as though some fury looking for its source

swept through & over us
clamping our mouths shut
& hemming us along a narrow trail.

LAWRENCE'S IRRITATIONS

He thrives himself
naked to the sungod, knows
those others in their rubbery ways
mere sunbathers, disintegrate in it—

it's an old truth known here & there he tells,
everyone
becoming Lawrence, among
everyone.

SONNET

If your child is holding you
in an intensity of feeling that you find's
too difficult to bear
you can abstract yourself by naming this
experience: Biological identity.
There is a use of category
that brings hopeless reassurance.

You think of big B Being,
with all that term can bear to you.
You needn't think it rimes with big B Boeing
in that rare realm where you are big G Going.
And call the boy your son.
This is a sonnet.

OH. AH, UGH

—the agony
of what they will not see.
The anger forces me
to be articulate against
these rimes that anger makes—

they write, I read, Oh
all they will not
let me see in what
each thinks he's seeing—

as fingers
strike the keys, the hands
at last located
no longer clutch

convulsively upon
themselves, as if
some idiot were there
ambiguously company.

AFTER BRECHT

Be thankful it's this dark.
Nobody knows what you're up to.
What if they did—
who's to say it's wrong.

Anything we want to do,
as long as we can find the energy,
we do it.   That's how come
it's getting darker all the time.

What if some dark night
they do you in. No last moments
marred by the injustice of it all.
I don't know who to thank.

THE PLOT

Christmas 6 feet deep.
Christmas 3 feet wide.
Christmas 6 feet long.
Stuffed with straw.

A DITTY

I was an identity
but the truth appears

we're no two souls alike
like snowflakes.

The truck had nearly struck their car. He had screamed. She had asked him not to.

If he fucked 2 women per night that would come to 730 in a year! But in 20 years that would only make 14600. He decided to retire. He was too quick at doing figures in his head. Then came the spring. Then came the fall.

The man whose path is blocked by his own frontal bone will forever lose himself in the precious arbitrariness of a particular arrangement of words. Power to the People, Robert David Cohen. But I don't know how to cut sugar-cane.

The boy kept shifting the objects on the meal-table, often no more than a fraction of an inch each time. This way no one would get hurt, least of all himself. As we watched we saw his reasoning. It drove the grownups to distraction & they invented an excuse to beat him. As we watched we saw his reasoning.

These were justified margins. Hitherto he'd been trapped between the other kind. He sighed with relief & a patch of white appeared in the dense grey of his face. He grew tense after tense but nothing would erase the blank white columns at either edge of his vision. He was as though chained to them. If this were real life he could bring the roof down but as it transpired he was merely booked & printed. These were unjustifiable measures.

He wondered why they were writing in lines. There **are**
reasons & reasons. Some are beneath consideration but some
are not above it. People walk because of their body-structure,
while they promenade to be seen. He's reminded of something
for which there was a reason: he's reminded of something.

His rhetoric was rich. The cake was richly crammed with
raisins, only nobody much eats christmas cake these days, &
that's their loss. The hilt of the sword was richly studded
with jewels. The attic was richly cluttered with junk.

Cancel contracts. Explanation follows. Description enclosed. Message concludes. Signature illegible. Never delivered.

It was delightful weather today. He had brought me his latest book. We sat on the porch & talked. That is what we were doing then. He asserted that writing wasn't the most important thing in life. We were bound to find ourselves at cross-purposes. He was sitting on the porch talking, & I am writing this.

If I go blind, will you read to me, he asked. He has very clear sight. He can see a long way. What would you like to hear, she replied.

It all, as he tells us, rests firmly on the edge of oblivion. Living on, we will not see his face again. I don't want to see what I shall never again see. That's why it all has to look permanent. I want to rest. He hasn't found rest, rest is a sentient occasion. He is permanent. I can alter his significance with every sentence.

Sitting in judgment on one's judgment. The wind moves by one in the grasses. How vague it is. How clear it might be. Who was one addressing. One's reflectiveness did one credit. Several possibilities occurred. One had recently left—someone who wouldn't allow one to be who one wanted, but rather, invented a person this someone wanted one to be. One hoped not to receive another such visit. One did not like to be alone.

We miss those things you used to make, when? It only seems like yesterday.

This then was the Zen Center. They had been kind enough to put him up overnight. He examined his cell. He tested the pallet on its floor. It was hard. He was not naif. He knew it was arranged so as to make him confront who he really was. He wanted a soft mattress & one of the Zen-women sent in.

A poem provides no one answer, but answers arise as one gets down to it.

A sentence, as the expression of a complete thought, is not natural & does not exist in nature. Is not natural & does not exist in nature.

Love is just around the corner. Any corner obscures one's view. Any corner constitutes one's view. Even if it's a tight one—you're fighting for your life. How not to believe it is a right angle, although any intersection consists of 4 such, facing various directions. Love is a dense volume. All its pages have corners. Sometimes, as here, only words can be the means to turn them.

The voice that came in the trance announced, People are here to hide the fact that we exist. It was a hard fact for people to believe, he found, because they didn't know who was relaying this information.

The comet is coming. Much happiness will attend this event. Kisses will mingle blood with blood. Pestilence will spread. Murder & mayhem will rage. And when the gutters of the city run with our wishes, the comet will have brought them in its train.

He had contracted cancer because he had lost the will to live. The one who knew this had not got cancer nor lost the will to live. The first man died. Now nobody could contradict him.

The novel is full of various anti-people notions which make the reader wonder whether the masses are capable of doing anything to protect their own interests. One of these notions is that workers have no scruples & will cross picket lines & cause hardship to their fellows for the sake of feeding their own families. This writer should get his nose out of his book & go take a look at what goes on.

He was a writer, & a popular one. People asked him what they should do. He could tell a good story. Once, he'd wanted to make it seem that the dining-hall had been wrecked. He was very drunk. Carefully, he thought, he took each chair & table & turned them upside down. In the morning, he woke to a satisfying buzz. The dining-hall *had* been wrecked.

He was flying at 20,000 feet because he'd boarded a plane at the airport. He was flying at 20,000 feet because conditions where he found himself supported such life as he was. He was flying at 20,000 feet because he'd been told so several minutes since. What was he doing on this plane? He was flying at 17,000 feet.

As she waded through & then up from the river, more of her skin became visible with each step. There was nothing remarkable about it, lovely as it was, but where the legs are joined to the trunk grew a roughly triangular shock of darkish hair. But the banks were full of people in a similar condition. The river however flowed between them.

Although the thin green stem led up to the flower, the flower opened wide & 3 layers of rose-colored petals were disclosed. Despite this, there were sharp projections all down the stem. He was filled with wonder, but blood was forming little globes at his fingertips.

It was the first creature of its kind to be found on Earth. Nor was it at all certain it had kin. It lacked genitalia & was more or less indescribable. She called it Fluke & kept it under the privy. If you wanted to look at Fluke, you would also see Willa's way of caring, & how she set out the dishes that might have been of liquid tar & blowing sand in full expectation of her love's return.

You never met anyone like me & you never will. How else could you know who I am. Who do you think you are. I've met your kind before.

He washed up on a desert island, where he experienced the most remarkable series of mishaps that somehow kept turning out for the best. He had no time to keep a journal. He was never rescued.

She said if she so desired she could go to any bar & know some one'd take her home & fuck her. But any man who went there couldn't be that sure. He might or might not score. That's the reason men take up such offers. She wasn't about to go out to any bar.

An evening like many he had spent, the lamps lit, a fire in the hearth, darkness at the windows, the moths fluttering at them. A white hair floated onto the typewriter. What was this utter sense of reassurance—none of this had ever happened before.

They sought, on the walls, a quantity of things that were not there, & ended by seeing them, but no longer knew the dates they represented.

Dates?

The branches grew at a certain angle in relation to the light. The trees bent away from the direction of the prevailing winds. He examined his fingers. Between each at the base was a small web from swimming. He brought them up close to his eyes. Now he could no longer see them. But between them he could still see the trees. They had a persistent quality. Soon it would be night.

How hard it is to speak of the death of love, if that is the death, & the emotion, I do speak of, here. There's an almost interminable search for the right word. And what makes it so difficult if not an equal determination not to disclose to oneself what the right word is. No choice is possible. One leaps, so to speak, & if (as is probable) one leaps forward, one will always land on one's face. To speak at all, so confronted, is to ensure that one or the other possibility wins out. There'll be a loss, also, roughly equal to the gain. There's no time to lose then, & I must begin as best I can.

I would be absolutely clear, at the outset, on one point: I'm a man who doesn't always get what he wants, but possessed of such determination & will-power that, I believe, had I wanted to be President, I would have come close. Others, luckier by birth, have done no more. Once I got the scent of some thing or person who could enable me to realize my desire, no further hindrances were possible to me, & to this day I'm capable of pursuing a line of action long after most would have seen reason & gone home. It may not seem odd, therefore, that I tell of this, but we blunder into grace as a thief into a safe, & that's a story in itself.

Hilda wasn't the first person I loved, but neither was she the last, & I select our story, I suppose, with some notion of a median in mind. Let me add that, in returning that love as she did, she introduced me to a complication, angry as it made me, that even now I'm hopeful may recur.

She was only passing through the town where then I lived, & this alone was sufficient to arouse the will of which I speak. Could I contrive to fall in love with her, or couldn't I, before the week was up? Even—or especially—if she felt no attraction toward me? Her person I found attractive, which should have helped, but then, how should it be otherwise. I knew what I wanted, while men will find beauty anywhere. But nothing brought the affair to a head more than Hilda's own will. By the second evening we were hopelessly desirous of going all the way, of finding ourselves utterly at one another's mercy; & she, after all, would be out of this place & into the safety of the next stop on her itinerary, as fast as the next plane could carry her.

I don't know if she was a virgin but I was, for the one girl who had taken pity on me before had bitten off more than she could chew, expecting no more than a casual roll in the hay where I was looking for something far more obtainable. This may be difficult to comprehend these days, but I see a terrible obscurity refused in contemporary relaxation. Naturally enough, then, when Hilda, in that actual hayloft, lay back, I knew what was wanted of me & I let my will have its way, so that, if her tour-guide hadn't shouted that I was to bring her to the house right away, I don't know what might not have happened. It might have ended then & there. But his indignation, & that of the entire group, was impressive, so that for the rest of her stay a tacit understanding—call it an irrational terror—kept us within its limits, & the romance flourished. And I had time to think things through.

If we fuck, I thought, we'll get what we want, & although that won't be the end of it, our commitment will be absolute & permission thus granted to the least desire the other might in all reason be expected to fulfil. This outweighed the claim I sensed in the alternative, namely, that to abstain from the ritual admitting us to such commitment opened the way to a rarer kind of love, scorn her as I would.

She wrote from her next stopover, with less ardor than I should have expected, & sensing in what she said, & even more, in what she didn't say, the fulfilment I was bent on, I quit my job—by then as tedious as anything one can do with one hand tied behind his back—& joined her. There, on a rock covered with slippery moss, she granted me a happiness I've never known either before or since, wriggling from her jeans to receive me in a way so unlike my imaginings that I came almost at once, initiated into this mystery with a swiftness that left me numb. It was achieved. From here on in, however in memory I'd try to violate her actual response, her calm acceptance would win out over my fantasies. Since puberty, or before, something in me had longed for this moment with this person, & that is what we mean by Fate. And

68

now I was satisfied there was no turning back. In fact we repeated the act once or twice before we parted, increasing our pleasure by the use of safes.

Hilda had topaz eyes, a face somehow all profile, hair, arms, legs—I will remember them all to my dying day, for who knows? This may be it. Against the vicissitudes of Chance there's only the human will, & if mine shows me those topaz eyes blurry with tears, this is more than the cat sees, for where are her kittens today? She cried because she had told me she loved me so much that she'd twice let me do something disgusting to her. Given the act was so repulsive to her, I was loved indeed, & in a way that assured me sooner or later she'd be able to look unflinchingly at what we had together in a way consonant with my own. And I could appreciate her duplicity, during the act (for if she kept herself to herself at such times, still, she hadn't actively rejected me); for I put it to myself that, if she couldn't be trusted at a time like that, she was hardly to be trusted now. Probably there'd been a pleasure taken in it which she was incapable of facing up to now.

But all reflection aside, she'd won my heart, & what time had we left for reflection? It was time for farewells—she was to fly back home tomorrow. Although I'd resolved never to let her go, I'd seen her ticket, & my distraction, trying to reconcile these apparently contradictory facts, caused me to act oddly. She'd just taken a shower, &, seeing her naked body next to the scales, I suggested she should weigh herself. Her refusal so surprised me that I grew insistent, but try as I might I couldn't push or lift her onto them. How ridiculous—what did she think to hide? It was already obvious she was a big girl. Later, I saw this was a lovers' tiff, & further evidence that we were lovers. I wouldn't go to the airport to see her off. Why prolong the agony. I had meant to go, but slept late. My subconscious knew what it was up to, & wisely exchanged the pain of parting for the pain of a small betrayal & the ensuing remorse. But after all, I'd seen an airport before, & I'd seen Hilda. How stupidly literal does one need to be.

She wrote once. I was chagrined to learn she wasn't pregnant, for I wanted some tangible form to grow from our relationship, heavy as it had been heavy. And too, I knew, I don't know how, that I had the makings of a real father. Still, I believe the real reason I didn't use a safe that first time, although there was one in my pocket all along, was that she'd have suspected my far-sightedness, with its demeaning implications concerning her powers of resistance, & that she'd have concluded from that that I was too clear-headed to be truly in love. Her contempt was not my object, or, if it was, my diffidence lost me that opportunity.

She said nothing in the letter concerning any infidelities. I took her blandness for dishonesty. Then, as if from nowhere, I was inspired to think that, after all, what was she to me? I saw that, if I didn't in fact love her, her letter would mean nothing to me. With this realization my strength returned, I was able to pick up the letter & re-read it several further times. I had to admit that, to an outsider, her prose was decidedly thin—how could one love such insipidity? Yes, but were it not for love, how would blandness make its way in the world. Instrumentality is everywhere, & I was relieved to find I had my part to play.

Hilda for now was out of reach, so I laid my plans. I had to save my fare, I had to find a job, I had to find a room. I did the last two & began to do the first. I settled back to make all I might of the next stage.

The mail came after I left in the morning so it was early evening before I could sort through the letters on the hallstand & find no news of Hilda. Each evening I hurried back to the boarding-house & scooped up my mail & ran up the stairs two at a time to reduce by several seconds the anticipated moment, which I see I delayed by not looking for an envelope with her writing on it until I was safely in my room, the door locked. Well, none of us is perfect. This I did five days a week for two months, my faith was unshakeable. What use to live wholly for the future. If we are to get what we want, now is the only time.

I had to suppose she was ill—had had an accident, was crippled, had lost a leg or an arm, some toes at least. Such thoughts caused me pain, though not, of course, as much as they were causing Hilda, if there's anything to telepathy. Of all the possi-

bilities, the one I most often had in mind was that she was para-
lyzed from the waist down. But as time went by, I saw others.
Sometimes I thought I could sit in that room forever thinking
about them but the excitement of getting the mail depended on
being away during the day. And the job was a constant humilia-
tion, & that too kept me occupied.

I could usually ignore my employer—he would speak harshly,
as if my errors were deliberate, but right or not, I knew I was
quitting soon, so little could mar my enjoyment of his censure,
impotent as it had to be. I had no time to finish any task he urged
me to begin, his upbraidings themselves being practically insur-
mountable interruptions. In my opinion he didn't have long to
live. That's why he projected his sense of defeat onto me, but he
wasn't really there at all as far as I was concerned, for I had my
love to keep me distant. True, if I was lonely before, I was lonely
now, so nothing had changed. But now I could think of Hilda, &
every detail of our time together. One day I rose to my feet &
began to kick everything in reach, in short order I'd smashed the
place, for I'd always known that where there's a will, there's a
way. It was that same evening I went over to Adrienne's for
what she termed "solace." She worked at the same place, & I'd
only been able to resist her by telling her how I'd sworn fidelity
to Hilda. Perhaps, since this made our relationship so much like
mine & Hilda's at this time, it was a kind of infidelity after all,
but I can't extract much satisfaction from that conjecture. Still,
if your reach doesn't exceed your grasp, why do the trees grow
fruit out of our reach?

Adrienne was a sympathetic listener, laughing when I said
that & similar things. And when I'd told her something of Hilda,
she had to respect my constancy, seeing that she wanted the same
for herself. Which all her protestations about loving me now &
without future designs could only make plain. This law of oppo-
sites was beyond her in her simple-mindedness, but, slow as she
was, she was bound to make some man satisfied, & I had to be
careful around her. As I discovered when, after spending my last
week in town on her floor—for my landlady had started to come
on to me too—I found myself, on the final night, in Adrienne's
bed. But that's another story, a story all in itself; & one very

much like this, so I don't have to tell it here. It was enough, that I would have that to confess to Hilda, when we met.

I couldn't afford a plane ticket, so I took the greyhound. What we cannot reach by flying, we must reach by limping, as I always tell myself.

A year had passed, & Hilda had grown some four or five inches, so she was now six feet or so; her wrists, that had been long with that vulnerability I find highly attractive, so that I'd fancy how she'd look, hung from a beam, were now much bonier, as though she *had* been. Her face had lost its bloom, & all in all, I found her ugly, pitifully so, & redoubled my efforts to act as though I were still under her spell. And in a sense I was. Consider my investment! To cut my losses now would be like cutting my fingernails or my hair.

So understandably I didn't for the first few minutes hear what she was saying. Which turned out to be that she had written me a second letter—upon receiving my last, that announced I was about to come to her—& she had sent it to the boarding-house. I suppose the landlady there destroyed it, in a jealous fit. And Hilda's letter had told me it was all over, she was engaged to somebody else. I saw almost at once that my love was to be tested as never before. I settled into my chair & gazed into her face. I was prepared to listen to her forever. Although I'm alone as I write of it, it's as though she sat across that table from me still, telling me what to put down. I lost her, true, but in the long run, what difference has it made? I am still capable of laying this story at her feet, or, if she won't open it, at her door. I take no credit for my strength of will. If it is stronger than love itself, surely it comes from the same mysterious place—for which I can't, somehow, find the right word. But if I could, wouldn't it lead to another, then another? There would be no way to stop. I was unable to stop with Hilda, & that naturally makes me not want to stop now.

9 PIECES FOR 9 VOICES INTERRUPTING 1 FOR NONE

1

When I take a walk with you
I take many 100 steps

then fall flat on my face.
This once I'll tell you why.

I am trying to alarm you
because I want to harm you.

That clears up a part of it,
but part remains a mystery:

the way that I restrain myself
& when I know to stop.

2

When I told you I enjoyed it
I felt disgusted with myself.

Truly it disgusted me
as I was afraid you'd see.

But I couldn't bring myself
to hurt you openly

so I told you it was great
in such a way I could be pretty sure

you'd find out later
differently, & I was right.

3

I am a student from Cambridge University,
you can tell a stranger

anything, that's why I love to travel.
Anonymity. Actually

I was working on a farm
having flunked 10th grade. He was

the owner of a restaurant.
And I believed him.

He would have liked me
anyway. Why, he didn't say.

4

The wind has no voice
except a poet fake it,

stoking his fire—
but that day when the wind

shifted as you shifted
so the smoke

was always blowing in your face
I'd gone too far. I hear

if I blow near where you are
that where there's smoke, & so on.

5

Something representing an intent
occurring where he reads it with

what one can call his paranoia
because he takes it to be true

infuses all behavior
—behavior all infuses

because he takes it to be true
what one can call his paranoia

occurring where he reads it with
something representing an intent.

6

If I'd come right out & said it
you'd have found out where you stood

unpleasant as it was
but I know a worser torment:

so I wrote it out
in code with just enough

by way of clues for you
to catch a hint I meant to

do you in. When you force me to confess this
I'll go along with you.

7

I got you to kiss me
so's I could hurt your wife,

I never liked her.
Why should she get to live with you.

Night after night she lies there
in my proper place—

how can I do you in
when she is in my way

& I always was aware how you admired me.
Even though you never got inside me.

8

Try as you might to hide it,
yours is a suspicious nature.

So we really had to work to set you up.
Lucky in love, lucky at cards, lucky

us to have at our disposal
all the secret agencies

of your experience—lucky
you, to have enjoyed so much.

But this is it. The way you knew
that it'd end. We've given up.

9

Now you know most all of it,
& us. Just how we suck you

dry. And why
we fuck with you

the way we do. Because
you're there. But once

you've seen through us
our usefulness is at an end.

So long. You're on your own
pretending we would like to phone.

76

He thought it humanity's lot for ever to be persuading a huge rock up a mountainside, & at the top it would roll back down the same side, unaided. Those who would disagree with him were at liberty to remark the beauty of the Alpine meadows, the whiteness of the Eidelweiss, & the unearthly peace of the pauses in this process, but not to deny they had rocks in their heads.

If the workers were alienated, their so-called betters were doubly so. The society in its deadly way dragged on & on & nothing could redeem it short of a spiritual revolution to put men & women in touch with their immediate needs, so that what came to hand would show one where one's head was at. Her guru, whose ruminations these sentences derive from, had performed one final miracle before dying, 30 years ago: he'd willed that no decay should disturb his well-loved form. Now she found herself in Tibet, cutting her guru's hair & finger-nails.

An angel stood before him in a vision & told him to catch the next number 67 bus. An inner voice announced it was time to plant the lettuce. On the bus he found a penny. This meant he was going to get money. In the penny a man's face appeared. He was going to be president. It was time to get off. A sound too high for human hearing assured him no birds would be flying today. A flock of birds flew past. This meant war, R,A,W, means war.

The unconscious is a station on the Metro. No trains ever stop there. That's why the platform is so crowded. Whenever he alighted there, he found it all attention. Something obscure was always vanishing, into the tunnel or out of it.

All the most brilliant periods of history flashed before his eyes as the sun glinted up off the sea. He was blinded momentarily & alone with some red & green dots & patches. But something that drummed in his ears reassured him. That was the ocean of his dreams.

Beauty is truth, they say. The boys sauntered up the driveway, & as they went they used their sticks to lop the blossoms off the irises lining it. They were talking about something else.

As it fell out, he fell out of the train he chanced to have caught, & by sheer good fortune landed in a passing river. He was fished out by a couple of picturesque gamekeepers who, unable to believe what their luck had brought them, realized he meant nothing to them & left him for dead on the bank. Here an occasional heiress revived him on a mere whim, not knowing what to make of him. Already his will was to make the truth of his life the purely arbitrary.

But expressiveness is a myth: it is only the convention of ex-pressiveness. How cold the real thing can sound.

The streets intersected at right angles. You might say they met. He did one time go through a wall, but that was to avoid the traffic cop. And on each corner, he saw a small semi-circle that meant 90 degrees. When it snows this is no longer visible. Then the man could have traced his steps.

Rosemary is an insidious herb. Its results are quite as predictable as those of alcohol. The twiggy stuff is crumbled between the fingers & it doesn't matter whose, death ensues. There was also the fear of others bumping into him. Now they would put their foot into the rosemary bush.

Higher intelligences are sending messages not to be thorough-
ly deciphered until the cataclysmic event they would save us
from shall occur. They live at the center of the galaxy while
human life is on the edge. Lower intelligences too are active,
& their messages are looking for some center.

It was in Leo & she was a Leo. It was hot. These men were
drawn to her by the power of that conjunction. Would she
give them away in September? They were getting to be an
irritant. She remembered to hunt for her medication. No-one
hereabouts dispensed it. She couldn't dispense with it. Now she
was getting warm. It was under the almanac.

When she returned home, nearly 2 hours after the time she'd told him to expect her, he was quickly aware of something different about her—some alteration in her accustomed manner so subtle & so elusive as to be evident only to him, though even he couldn't put his finger on it quite yet. I've been fucking Ben, she said.

When she returned home, surely it was at least 2 hours after the time she'd named, he was aware, almost as though he'd expected it, of some subtle change in her accustomed manner, though only he, her husband of many years, would notice it, he supposed, as he studied her narrowly for the one clue more he needed. I haven't been fucking Ben if that's what you think, she said.

When she returned home, he studied her for some minutes, covertly, puffing on his meerschaum & with his other hand thrust deep into his dressing-gown pocket. His lean, hawklike features were a sight to see. I got my hair done, she told him.

But now he had a rash on his hawklike penis.

She is sleeping. He raises the pillow & holds it just above her mouth & nostrils. Such thoughts race through his head as can't be put into words. People shift uneasily. Who knows what he'll do next. He's forgotten his lines.

Everywhere he went he thought of her. Everything he did he did differently because of her. He could hardly wait for the next time. Wasn't this the doing of the god Amor? Now he had forgotten her phone number.

3 people whom she knew were coming up the lane. The sun was just setting. Their car stopped at the stop sign. Now, as the wind got up, all the trees began to whisper. One of them knew these people she knew elsewhere, where she had lately been, who had the treehouse. Now it grew dark. It was all a coincidence.

Light is a shower of pebbles. Light is a shower of ripples. Light is a sower of parables. Light is a sewer of symbols. Light is right & white & might & sight, light has an endless appetite, until it looks like night.

Her mother was an archetype if ever there was one.

The archway dissolved as his eyes went out of focus. Anything sight could do, men would find out how to.

He put his hand on her. He put his hand on her. He was con-
fused. He is not to be confused with someone else.

He felt, sometimes apologetically, that he'd had a happy child-
hood. Then they told him about the isolation hospital. In 5
minutes his happy childhood had been wiped out. Now he be-
gan to understand something about the way he was.

The 70's are the 50's all over. I recall in the 50's a number of
men who called their wives Mom. And I heard this again lately.

He put his hand to his mouth. He tore at the cuticles with his teeth. There was always a part that was missing in these descriptions. It was a hell of a way for 2 men to carry on.

He was a man about medium height, in his middle years, with carefully-bitten fingernails, but his shoes were dusty. The dam has burst he said.

There are no spiders on Jupiter. It is not possible to spin webs there. I used to read the newspaper.

I say everything you're thinking. I have no thoughts of my own.

Since poetry wasn't exactly fun they would make it look like a lot of fun in order to attract more readers of poetry. I have the form right here. But poets are evidently as poor at selling as they are at writing columns. As far as mass circulation's concerned, this is based on a faulty hypothesis. One has no choice but to cut corners.

The sun's heat made life possible on earth. The distance between sun & earth made life possible. There was a lot to write about.

There's always a way out. Everything is. If that's your trip, that is. Why not. Chance rules. God will provide. Luckily. There are many more.

Everything that was done was perfect. There was no room for judgment to move. Only a certain blind spot prevented people from discovering this single flaw.

When all's said & done, he could do one of 2 things.

He proposed that they could agree on one point, namely, no 2 persons can share an identical knowledge of the thoughts & feelings of either one. His companion rejected this proposition. His companion regarded him suspiciously. Then his companion started to laugh. He laughed & he laughed. How could they disagree.

Everyone got what they deserved—everyone.

The caves were opening in the surface of the earth. Their flashlights revealed the walls, the so-thought roof, the surface of the underground lake. The battery burned out & he turned & kissed her liver.

He had learned a new chord. Now he could play "Annabel Lee". No notes had been added to the piano. Yet there he was, in a kingdom by the sea. It was E flat minor.

Night found him in a strange place. What was close to him, suddenly was unfamiliar. There were sounds, nothing distinct. In among the trees was pitch black, oddly attractive. He looked away to where the ghost of light was, "up" as we say, & there sure enough were the stars, disposed as he thought in something like orders. Night had found him in a strange place.

Everywhere he went he thought of her. 3 people whom she knew were coming up the lane. He brought them up close to his eyes. They had a persistent quality, & each was a wire, reverberating. We can send someone in your place, they assured him. He might or mightn't score, & that's the reason men take up such offers. She had asked him not to.

He put his hand on her. He examined his fingers. He was confused. Between each at the base was a small web from women. Appealing as he found a number of people, not one but turned out discomfortingly apposed making him feel all thumbs. Wasn't this the doing of the god Amor? The closet was wet. What was this utter sense of reassurance—none of this had ever happened before.

We are taking it apart. Are you going to take a part. What part
are you anyway & don't you have a way to go. To depart is to be
in the way, in the way of being apart. Are we as partial to this
plot as I am partial to you. Then, aren't we partners till death
parts us. When the mortal part, that the plot parts to admit,
departs, is there a part left. This is part of what we are going
to take apart to give it a way. Part of our lot is art. If you are
going to take up an art & give it a lot, it's got to be taken apart,
that's part of the plot we take to be our lot. What part isn't a
way pointing to a common lot, what allotment, not a pointer to a
common plot. Without a common lot, what plot allots parts to
each, what imparts ways to plot such parts as we, you & I. We
are not partial to a pilot whose plane is a plan he is not in. A
pilot who's a Pan urges importunate puns in the name of Apollo
who parrots the pilot in a limited way. Part of the plot to be
taken apart & alloted a way allows that as the waves part, love
will depart the glottal depths & no longer be a presence apart,
thickening the plot, blotting out such parts as you & I, in loyalty
to the lottery, & the habit of commitment.

The initial wrench is sickening, unbelievable. How can this be happening to me. Maybe it's a defense against this to remember it, within a very short time, as utterly predictable, the inevitable culmination of a fateful series of acts. Possibly one will believe one willed it.

The pain is such that one won't want to move from the place where it happened, & will hug the hurt, pulling it into oneself. But it's most quickly alleviated if you get up & walk so that the injured part is forced to function. Soon only a sinister clicking within predicts the next stage.

Which is, a growing soreness & intractability, that will fix it in whatever position one adopts, which will usually be sitting, discussing how it happened probably, so that it grows increasingly difficult to straighten it out. But it must be straightened out in order to be bound so one can get around.

But more immediately, extreme cold affords relief. Something like an ice-pack, administered by a cool-headed friend, whose attentions may also ease the ego, which is wounded because one has been foolish enough to have this accident at all. The swelling however makes the friend hard to attend to.

Then it must be bound. This is what is always done in such cases. Which means that many, many others have had to endure pain of this kind. And they are now walking around okay, so, recovery looks to be highly probable. This bandage, which has to be elastic, supports the injured member & diminishes feeling therein.

But not entirely. At night, particularly, the efforts, to accomodate oneself to the hurt, place unaccustomed strain on other areas, making sleep as difficult as it is desirable. In the half-awake half-asleep state one may wonder whether these secondary pains aren't the cause of the first.

But one will wake up & start to think again. One may see how the incident could have been avoided. If the pain gets too intense one has recourse to drugs. One recalls how it has happened as it happened & it's best to forget all that entirely. One recalls friends who were intensely into drugs.

A doctor will draw off the excess fluid with a hollow needle, hollow because it's to be filled with one's own effluent. He won't use anesthetic, because the patient must advise him whether the needle is probing into the fluid, or the injured tissue itself. This shrinking procedure doesn't guarantee that fluid won't gather again. Then the procedure must be repeated. What's more, the doctor's bill will be repeated. And the doctor may not know what he is doing.

Twenty-four hours have passed. Now the compresses should be changed from cold to hot. Hot pads hasten the re-absorption back into the general body, of the blood & lymph instrumental in the swelling. Gentle massage may do the same. But if the injured member is subjected in this way to any stress, it will give way immediately.

After a while the patient will have found various ways of thinking about all this. I was trying to get to first base & I did, but I forgot it's the one base you're allowed to overrun, so I tried to stop there, & part of me did, but part kept right on going. Equally, everything one thinks of, to cover it up, will bring the wrench to mind.

As the experience enters one's repertoire, one will be able to advise others likewise afflicted. But the distance between one & one's own pain, a distance that increases of necessity, if one's ever to trust the injured part, must take something away from these sympathetic efforts. Little more appears possible than to state that softball has rules, & that a knee, also, is a working set of limitations.

A knee has limitations inherent in its function. It's a joint, where two bones are bound together by an unlikely cluster of tendons. These enable the leg to go places neither the calf nor the thigh could get to on their own. And when thigh & calf must go their separate ways, these can tear.

YOUR GIFT

In the genital embrace
the face
changes—

memory
surrenders its tumescence
to the act—

if afterward
one of the two
remember a commitment

to be elsewhere
with another similarly held,
both falter, so their masks

resume the proper functions,
& why suppose the eyes
do not alter too, to see a threat

each must reject—& judgment
must return
to its defense.

I see the way your chin
grew determined at the phone
you spoke into to tell me it was over.

I see your face
strong enough to soften & suffuse
with gifts of love

returned. Then love it is shows how
I am dead to you
as the you of my desire

has gone from me—
& to kill this vision
I would die to love,

recalling all that's gone
as empty words
can never come to life,

the grief
releasing us in me
refused & nothing of us left

except you show me
my divided will
chose, &

you were for me
as long as I desired you
strong enough.

A PRAYER

Make me a swine—
the wish
is only swinish

& Circe's is
her spell. Though
she's not here

her agent is
this memory
that roots

particulars
concerning fixities
that once were her

pubis, nostrils,
thighs, a mouth
with eyes—it's

dumb & blind
I see & say
so to possess

what then drives off
what's not
yet lost, since

all of it possesses
me as present
fantasy, possessed

still in my memory
that must,
apparently, refuse

its details any way
whereby either they
or Circe may

become mere words to all
I want to tell,
to create again the woman

whose beautiful
opacity I'd glimpsed
& opened to—

when hope, that she
might to desire prove
merciful,

closed on that glimpse
so that there pulsed
what that once made

a man of
what I
evidently am.

STILL THERE

The night mysterious with heat.
Its sky huge now with stars.
The people sprawled in little groups

Their voices quiet yet audible,
what do they say. These constellations
are indistinguishable from where we sit.

A slight wind murmurs in the cypresses
set there to turn it back. How black.
The distances among the clusters

are wildoat grass the sun's rays slowly leave.
What do we know. It ceases,
others come to see as much as we.

Those stars are me,
these sounds. Tears blur
& bring them to a field of points.

ITS END

They all had heard a rumor
that some body ultimate in its discretions
might be about to bloom
despite their heavy care. I
found I was among them, you
came to trouble me
with curiosity, blossoming
with my attention like the flowering plum—

I'd been thinking of you for a long time.
I knew you wanted love
Knew you'd heard the rumor
I knew you wanted me, I thought
how we could fuck
& that was bound to bring me to the place
where I just breathed
& touched & saw & heard you
once I'd found out by your mouth
how thinking of you tastes.

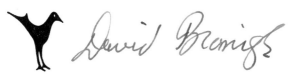

*Printed June 1974 in Santa Barbara for the Black
Sparrow Press by Noel Young. Design by Barbara
Martin. This edition is published in paper wrappers;
there are 200 copies numbered & signed by the poet;
& 26 lettered copies handbound in boards by Earle Gray
each with an original drawing by David Bromige.*

200

PHOTO: SAM JAFFE

David Bromige has moved around more than he cares to detail. His partial list is: London, England (his birthplace), 1933-49, 1957-58; N. Battleford, Saskatchewan, 1949, 1953-55; Bjuv, Sweden, 1952-53; Edmonton, Alberta, 1955-56; Vancouver, B.C., 1956-57, 1958-62, 1964; Berkeley, Calif., 1962-64, 1964-70; Sebastopol, Calif., 1970 to present.

He attended Haberdashers' Aske's (Hampstead) School for Boys, The Berkshire Institute of Agriculture, The University of British Columbia (BA '62), & UC Berkeley (MA '64).

He's earned his own living (with help from wives & grants) since 1951. At present he teaches at California State, Sonoma.

His sister lives in Vancouver. His father lives in London. His son Chris (b. 1964) alternates between Berkeley and Sebastopol. Bromige's present wife is Sherril Jaffe.

Sebastopol is a small town (pop. 4000) an hour's drive north of San Francisco. Safeway is in the business of acquiring it. What we call myth is the arrangement of the incidents.